COMING HOME

from the life of
Langston Hughes

FLOYD COOPER

The Putnam & Grosset Group

To my mother, Ramona Cooper

Book design by Nanette Stevenson and Donna Mark.
The text is set in Janson. Lettering by David Gatti.

"Hope" from *Selected Poems* by Langston Hughes, Copyright © 1942 by
Alfred A. Knopf, Inc. and renewed in 1970 by Arna Bontemps an George
Houston Bass. Reprinted by permission of the publisher.

Library of Congress Cataloging-in-Publication Data
Cooper, Floyd. Coming Home: from the life of Langston Hughes /
written and illustrated by Floyd Cooper. p. cm.
1. Hughes, Langston, 1902-1967—Biography—Juvenile literature.
2. Afro-American poets—20th century—Biography—Juvenile literature.
I. Title. PS3515.U274Z6178 1994 818'.5209—dc20
[B] 93-36332 CIP AC ISBN 0-698-11612-7

20 19 18 17 16 15

Hope

Sometimes when I'm lonely,
Don't know why,
Keep thinkin' I won't be lonely,
By and by.

Langston Hughes

James Langston Hughes was a dreamer, there in Lawrence, Kansas, where he lived alone with his Granma Mary Langston. Langston was a dreamer in the fields behind the two-room house he shared with her. Or on the porch.

His grandma didn't much like him playing with the neighborhood kids, so he'd hear kids playing ball or riding bikes, but he'd stay put.

Mostly in his early years, James Langston Hughes was alone.

Unless the distant faint familiar sound of a freight train pressed against his ears. Then Langston would bolt off the porch, hit the ground running, chickens aflutter. Quick! past the woodshed. Swoop! around the pump for drawing water.

He'd hurry across the vacant lot and through the wheat field. He'd run and run until between breaths, he could see the big freighter pulling its load around the curve of tracks, whistle blowing sweet, as it screeched and clanked: clackedy, clackedy, clackedy. The old rusty cars talking, talking.

The old iron snake'd tell him its stories about the places it'd been. Langston would talk back. Dream back. He'd dream of riding the train to Mexico where his pa, James Nathaniel Hughes, went to live after they wouldn't let him be a lawyer in Oklahoma because he was a black man. He'd dream of riding to where his ma, Carrie Hughes, was trying to be an actress on stage. He loved going to the theater with her those times he'd had the chance to be with her.

Mostly, he dreamed of the three of them together, of having a home with his ma and pa. A home he would never have to leave.

But each time the train would trail off, getting quieter and quieter, and quieter still, engine smoke barely clinging to the blue sky before it disappeared; Langston's dreams disappeared, too.

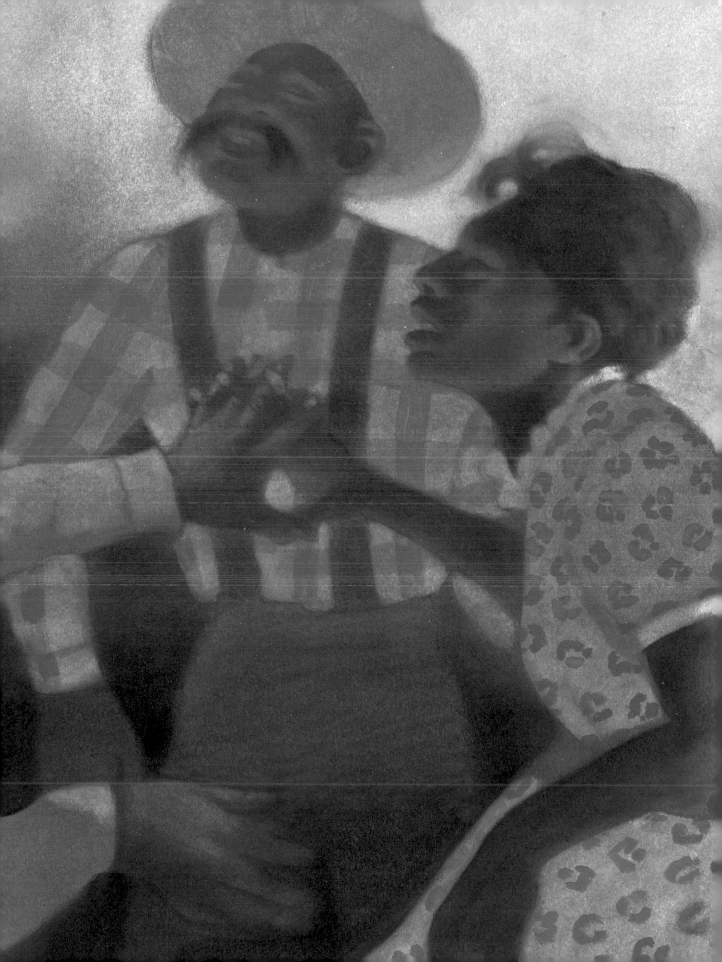

Living with Granma wasn't easy. She was poor. Dinner was often dandelion greens and whatever the neighbors passed over the back-yard fence. Sometimes the neighbors passed clothes, too, their used dresses, worn shirts, and old shoes.

Once Langston had to wear a woman's shoes, because his grandma couldn't buy him new ones.

But Granma believed a boy needed heroes, and one day she took Langston all the way to Topeka to hear Booker T. Washington speak. Booker T. Washington in person!

And she would read to young Langston—and storytell. Sometimes she'd read from the Bible. Other times it would be a beautiful tale from the Brothers Grimm.

Almost always, his grandma told stories of heroes. Heroes who were black, just like Langston.

His grandma's first husband, Lewis Sheridan Leary, had ridden with John Brown and was killed in the struggle to free slaves. She still wore his torn, bullet-riddled shawl.

Even on warm summer evenings she'd pull the shawl over Langston and tell him stories of her first husband, and of two uncles who were Buffalo soldiers, named that by the Indians because of their curly hair, and called the "bravest of the brave." And about Langston's uncle, John Mercer Langston, the first black American to hold office. He was a lawyer and later elected to Congress.

His grandma herself had worked on the Underground Railroad, helping slaves flee north to freedom, and she told him those stories.

Langston would hear these stories over and over. Wrapped in the torn shawl—and wrapped in family stories of pride and glory—he'd listen and dream.

Sometimes Langston's dreams about having a family came true. Like the time he, his ma, and grandma really did go to Mexico to see his father. Maybe, finally, Langston would have a home of his own.

But on April 14, 1907, the ground in Mexico began to tremble. Everything shook, including the building they were in. Langston's pa, carrying Langston, led everyone out into the street.

Everywhere walls of buildings cracked and split open. Giant tarantula spiders scurried out of the cracks. That was enough for his mama. As soon as the trains were running again, she and his grandma and Langston climbed back on the train and rode back to Kansas. Langston whispered a goodbye to Mexico, his father, and to having a home of his own.

Sometimes Langston's ma would send for him. He'd ride the train to the Kansas City Bottoms where she'd meet him and off they'd go. They'd see plays, the opera, and visit the library, where Langston was fascinated by the big, bright, silent reading room, the long smooth tables, and librarians who would so kindly get books for him.

Sometimes, when she was busy, his mother would leave him at his uncle Des's barbershop. He liked it there, right in the center of the black district. He'd go and wander the nearby streets. Speak to folks passing by. A nod here. A hat-tip there.

But mostly Langston would listen.

He'd ride his ears around the city. Through Market Street where everyone sang the song of haggle. Down side streets filled with kids who ran and played forever. Up the block where clubs and dance halls played jazzy old blues music that drifted down the alleys and tickled his soul. Langston felt the rhythms.

Other times Langston's ma would come to Lawrence. Once it wasn't the best of times for her. Money was scarce. She snapped at Langston and it hurt.

Later that evening they went to St. Luke's Church where Langston's ma was giving a performance. She told him that she had a wonderful surprise for him. That he was going to be on the stage with her. That he was going to be a star, just like she was going to be.

Langston didn't like the surprise. That evening he was the one with the surprise. As his ma introduced him, behind her back Langston made faces: He crossed his eyes, stretched his mouth, and imitated her. Everyone burst out laughing. The more people laughed, the more faces he made.

Embarrassed, his mother rushed off stage.

As Langston's grandma got on in years, she grew more and more silent. Then the time came when she hardly spoke at all. The little home where he had lived so long was quiet and lonely, with Granma rocking silent in her rocking chair.

A real home seemed less than ever like something Langston would ever have.

Then he went to live with friends of the family across town, Auntie and Uncle Reed, he called them.

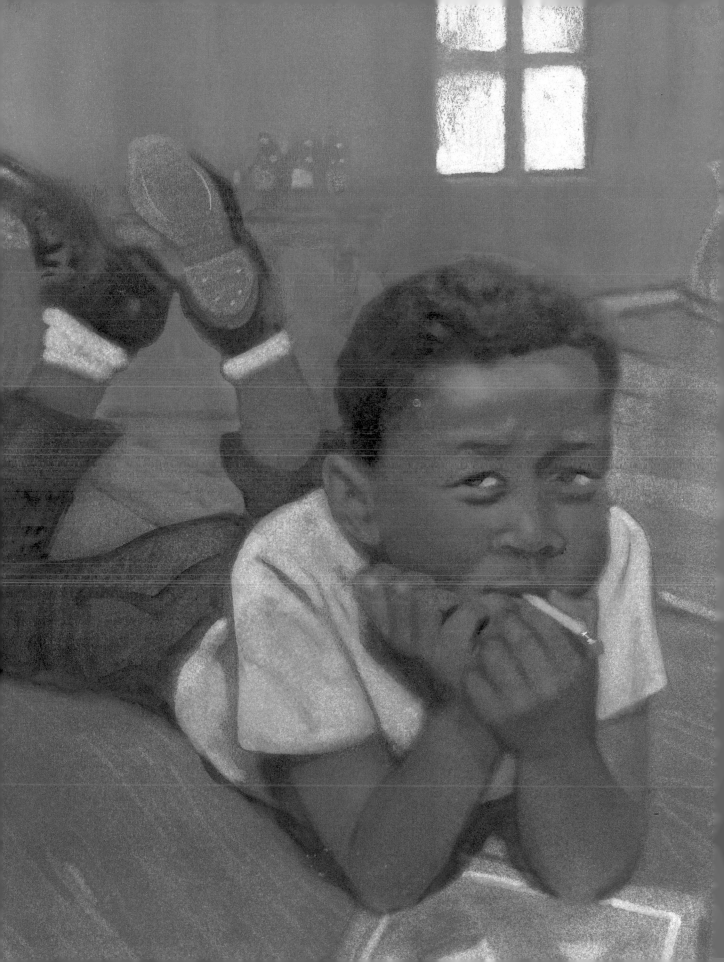

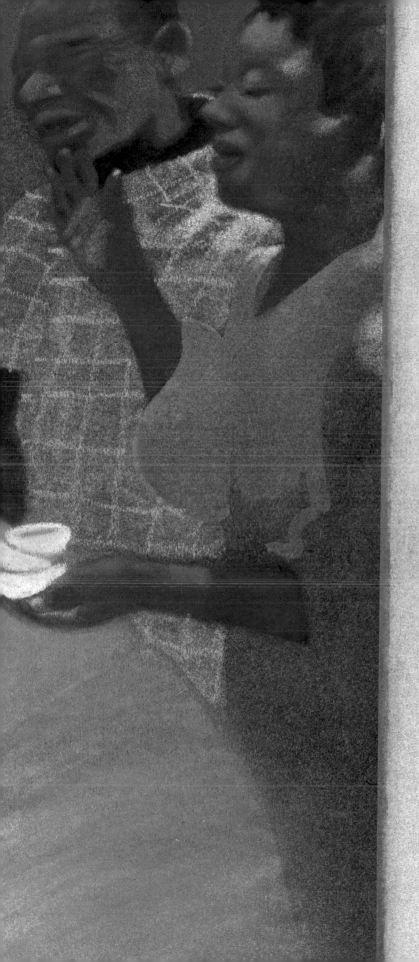

When Langston first saw the dinner table at the Reeds' he had never seen so much food in his life. After the blessing, Uncle Reed smiled and told Langston to eat up. He didn't have to tell Langston twice. Then Auntie, in a voice as sweet as dessert, said there was more out in the kitchen.

Langston soon learned that there would always be "more" from Auntie and Uncle Reed. More food, and more hugs and love.

On Sundays Auntie Reed would take Langston to church. He'd never gone before. Auntie Reed's church was all right, but in time Langston preferred the Baptist church down the street. The singing and preaching felt so familiar —like the rhythms of the streets in Kansas City. The words seemed to roll out of the preacher's mouth like jazzy old blues.

He had trouble understanding what everyone was feeling when they felt God, but he liked being there.

By now, Langston had grown popular at school, was thought of as "smart," and chosen class poet. He had begun writing poetry and sharing it. One of his first poems was "When Sue Wears Red," about a girl he admired in school. And then he wrote "Just Because I Loves You" and "The Negro Speaks of Rivers."

Now after school, he'd run and play with friends. Sometimes afterward they'd gather around Langston on the Reeds' front porch. There in the dark shadows of a summer night, Langston would tell stories.

Of the time he stood ten feet from Booker T. Washington, of his two uncles who were Buffalo soldiers, the "bravest of the brave." Of John Mercer Langston, the U.S. congressman. About his grandma's first husband who was killed with John Brown trying to free the slaves, and of Granma herself who used to work on the Underground Railroad.

Stories of real heroes who were black, just like Langston.

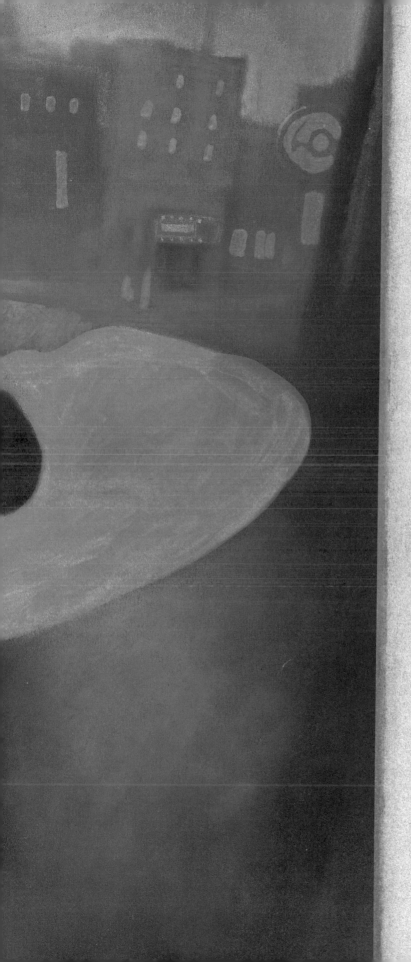

It grew clearer to Langston in those days what home really was. Life with his grandma had never been exactly like home. Life with his ma and pa never had been home, as much as he wanted it to be. Life with his Auntie and Uncle Reed felt like home, it smelled like home and looked like home. And home was all of the things the Reeds' home was.

But home was something more for him.

For him, home was a blues song sung in the pale evening night on a Kansas City street corner. Home was the theater where his ma performed, the library where he sat quiet, reading the books he loved. Home was the church, alive with music, where everybody was "brother" and "sister."

As he grew older, Langston Hughes wrote more and more. About everyday people, common folk. He wrote about dancers and children, troubled people and people in love; Walt Whitman and the black Pierrot; all kinds of people. And he traveled all over the world, to Russia and France, and to Africa, experiencing the stories and rhythms of yet other people.

He lived in many cities in America, like Cleveland and Los Angeles, but Harlem, New York, where all kinds of black artists gathered—writers, painters, musicians—became the place where he stayed longest and that he knew best.

It seemed Langston Hughes had finally found a home.

But the truth is, Langston never had a home like most people. Home was in him. And it was about his black family that he wrote in words that reached his own people, and all kinds of people of different races and different countries, all over the world.

AUTHOR'S NOTE

Langston Hughes, born February 1, 1902, in Joplin, Missouri, was a remarkable man. He survived a lonely childhood to become an internationally known writer and poet, a man known for his humor and compassion. A prominent writer of the Harlem Renaissance, he wrote poems, travel stories, and pieces of fiction, including the famous stories of Simple, the so-called "Everyman of his people."

Hughes came from distinctive lineage. On his mother's side he came from Indian, French, and African ancestry; his grandmother Mary was born free in North Carolina and attended college in Ohio. His grandfather, son of a Virginia planter and former slave, attended Oberlin Preparatory School. Both were active abolitionists. Langston's great-grandfathers on his father's side were prominent Kentuckians, one related to the statesman Henry Clay. Hughes's own father earned two teaching certificates.

Lawrence, Kansas, where Hughes grew up, was itself a unique city. Founded by abolitionists in 1854, it became a center of antislavery activity, and the black people who came there lived in a society where churches, hotels, restaurants, and theaters were open to both races. An attack by William Quantrill and his raiders in 1863 destroyed black-owned businesses and homes, and Lawrence was never again the same. Segregation had arrived. People like Mary Langston were understandably bitter.

Langston himself suffered some of the stings of segregation. When his mother took him to first grade at a nearby school, he was told he had to go across town to the school for "colored children." His mother fought this and won. But the children in the school did not let him forget he was a black boy in an all-white school. The schools in Lawrence were no better.

But at an early age, his teachers recognized his intelligence, and by the time he joined his mother in Lincoln, Illinois, in 1915, he had begun to write verse.

I have always thought of Langston Hughes as a beacon for all dreamers. For me, dreams spawn hope, and from hope springs life. When he died in 1967 at the age of 65, he left his stories and poems living on as an example to all, even those who have lost hope. Hopeless is homeless! And so, Langston beckons us all home.

Floyd Cooper

BIBLIOGRAPHY

Arnold Rampersad. *From the Life of Langston Hughes: Vol. I: 1902–1941: I, Too, Sing America*, New York: Oxford University Press, 1986.

Mark Scott. "Langston Hughes of Kansas," *Kansas History: A Journal of the Central Plains*, 3: 3–25, Spring, 1980.

Selected Poems of Langston Hughes, Vintage Classics Edition, New York: Random House, Inc., 1990.